MINIMUM **DESIGN**

Series directed by
Andrea Branzi

Tom DIXON

Davide Fabio Colaci and Angela Rui

24 ORE Cultura

Cover
S-Chair, Cappellini, 1991
Courtesy of Cappellini, Meda

Published by
24 ORE Cultura srl

Editorial Director
Natalina Costa

Project editor
Chiara Savino

Project Manager
Chiara Giudice
Anna Mainoli

Director of Production
Maurizio Bartomioli

Graphic design and page layout
Irma Robbiati

Picture research and editing
Silvia Russo

Photolithography
Valter Montani

Editorial assistant
Giorgia Montagna

Translation
Sylvia Adrian Notini

First edition: September 2011

ISBN 978-88-6648-002-0

Printed in Italy

MINIMUM **DESIGN**

Titles in the series
Gio Ponti
Franco Albini
Joe Colombo

Forthcoming titles
Alvar Aalto
Ron Arad
Gae Aulenti
Mario Bellini
Andrea Branzi
Achille e Pier Giacomo Castiglioni
Antonio Citterio
Michele De Lucchi
Stefano Giovannoni
Konstantin Grcic
Vico Magistretti
Angelo Mangiarotti
Enzo Mari
Alessandro Mendini
Carlo Mollino
Jasper Morrison
Eero Saarinen
Ettore Sottsass
Philippe Starck
Marco Zanuso

CONTENTS

Tom Dixon

Andrea Branzi

Trying to understand Tom Dixon's world, his personal way of designing and producing an object, is an interesting task because, unlike most of his contemporaries, nothing is left to "chance," and everything *is* a "chance." In many ways Tom Dixon is an excellent representative of England at the start of the 21st century: post-Beatles London, post-Tony Blair politics, Richard Rogers and Norman Foster's huge projects worldwide; the Britain of the ever-present dandy and the anarchists. But also the age-old British penchant for *pragmatism* as well as the phenomenon (an absolutely enviable one) of youthful creativity and a national economy of music…

Let's start with *pragmatism* as it can perhaps explain all the rest. Many of my British friends (like Peter Cook) believe that *pragmatism* means the *absence of Philosophy*; but pragmatism is actually a very precise *philosophy* (see Dewey and Rorty); pragmatism says that ideas are at the service of real life, and therefore that the validity of an idea does not lie in its intrinsic truth, but rather in its operative force. Thoughts are instruments that help us along our existential pathway. So we really are talking about a philosophy, perhaps an empirical one, one that's more down-to-earth than others, certainly more suited to a seafaring and ex-colonial population distrustful of ideological overloads (no room on board) and abstract ideas that can't be verified. In the wonderful books he has written, *Rethink* (London 2000) and especially *The Interior World of Tom Dixon* (London 2008), the designer suggests, without actually actually coming out and saying it, that "the world already exists and it's a question of using it as best possible, even to change it." His books are lengthy and brilliant perusals of the technology, products, materials, existing mechanisms that can be used for applications that are different, smarter and farther-reaching. The term "Interior World" can thus be understood as a space that's located inside, but also as the *innermost* space of a very sophisticated designer, who wishes to free the world from useless superstructures and the wasting of mental energy. Dixon's books do not merely promote his own projects; they illustrate his intelligence and aptitude for exploring, studying, investigating the potential of the real world in order to create another perhaps realer one (a popular sport with the British, an example of which could be Per Mollerup's book *Collapsibles. A Design Album of Space-Saving Objects*, London, 2001, dedicated to all the stackable, foldable, articulated and modular objects in the world).

Tom Dixon, like many other European designers, began his career working in Italy, especially with Giulio Cappellini (who has always been a superb talent scout) because he found here the consolidated tradition of small- to medium-sized enterprises that hold a dialogue with creative logic. But in 2002, truly the pragmatist, Tom Dixon founded a *self-brand*, as if to demonstrate that his projects were useful to others but more importantly to himself. Other designers followed suit (Giorgetto Giugiaro, Michele De Lucchi and the Dutch members of Droog Design, among others), and went from being simple *de-

signers* to *self-entrepreneurs*. This phenomenon is typical of the new globalized economy, where it's less important to own a *factory*, and much more important to have *ideas, industrial* projects and strategies. The distance that at one time existed between entrepreneurial culture and the culture of the project has been whittled down: to be able to deal with international competition an industrialist has to know how to manage the continuing innovation of his own supply and his own image; the designer is someone who provides this type of innovative energy. So these two destinies are now coming together in a sort of historical alliance.

But Tom Dixon, again thanks to his pragmatism, didn't allow himself to be trapped inside the limited role of explorer of existing technologies (in 2007 he founded Design Research Studio), or in that of the self-employed businessman; rather, he participated in the wave of creativity that started out in London and invaded the world through music.

Tom Dixon, who once played the bass guitar with Funkapolitan (and who even looks a lot like Tom Waits), began to design objects that were sweet and harmonious, much like the riff played by an electric guitar: objects that seem to be born from the mysterious and ancient skill of British soldiers to enthrall the world with their wartime songs. Unlike Italian design, which in most cases emerges from an idea and then seeks the materials needed to make it, Tom Dixon instead starts from the tools, the materials, the technology available, and by combining all these ingredients he creates objects that are very different, but all of which characterized by a sort of ironic capacity to challenge the unthinkable, the unforeseeable, and forever discover more and more pleasurable accords.

5

66 Some days I work as a designer,
but the bits that really interest
me are the invention, engineering and
marketing rather than
the actual process of designing.
I think that effective designers tend
to be interested in the whole chain.
I'm a designer very occasionally.
I tend to be on the periphery,
occasionally popping out a product
which is designed mainly through
an interest in materials
and technologies. 99

Peg Chair, 2010

EXT REM ISM

Tom Dixon

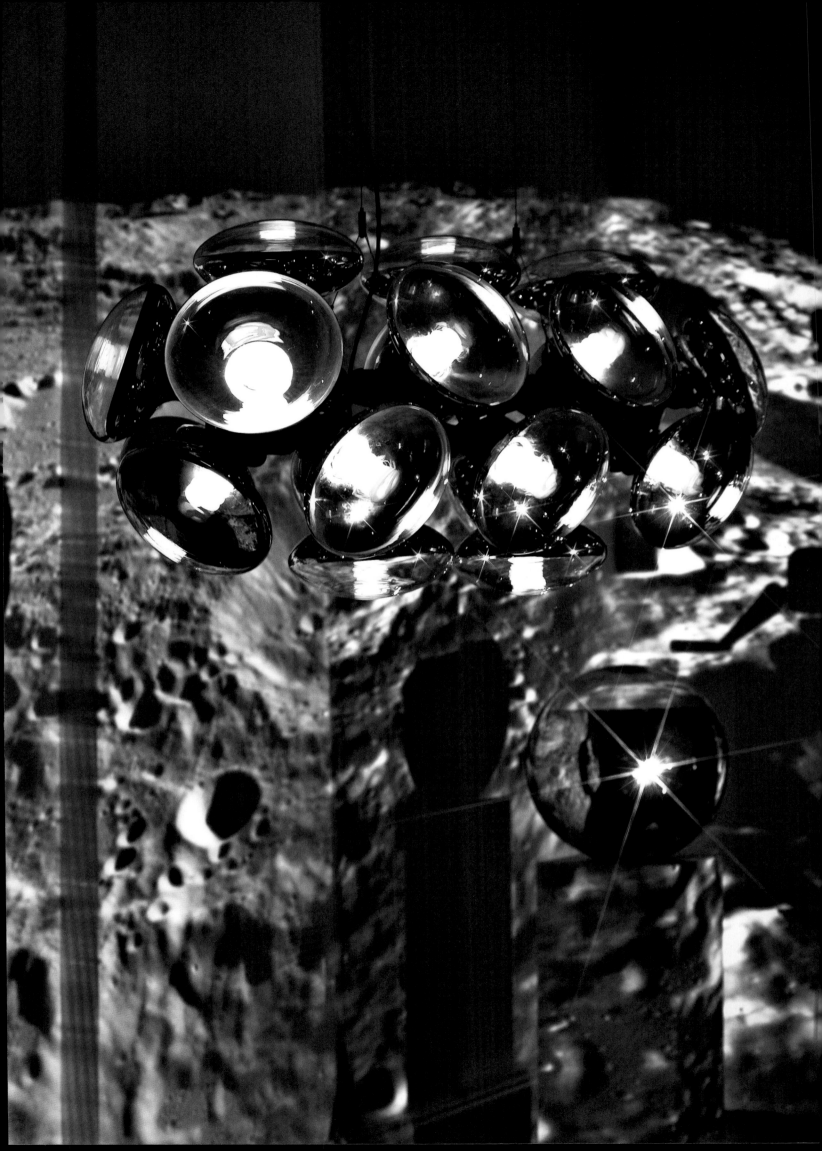

Indigo Fan Chair, 2011

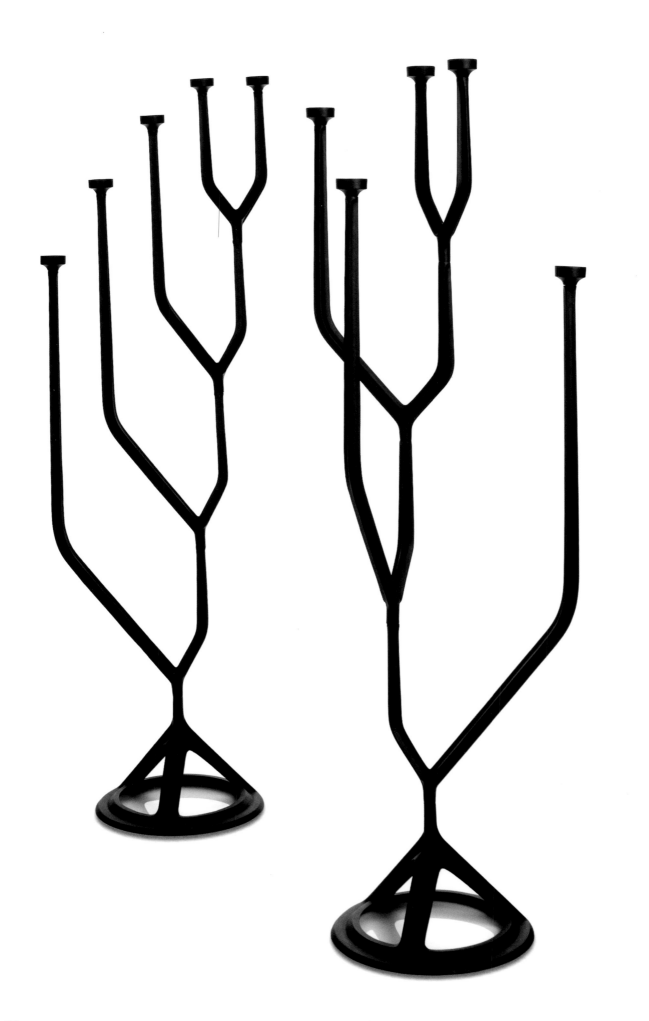

Clockwise, candelabra:
Spin Floor, 2007,
Crown, 2009,
Spin Table, 2006

pp. 24-25
Black and white Jack
Lights, 2010

pp. 26-27
The Great Light
Giveaway in Trafalgar
Square, London, 2007

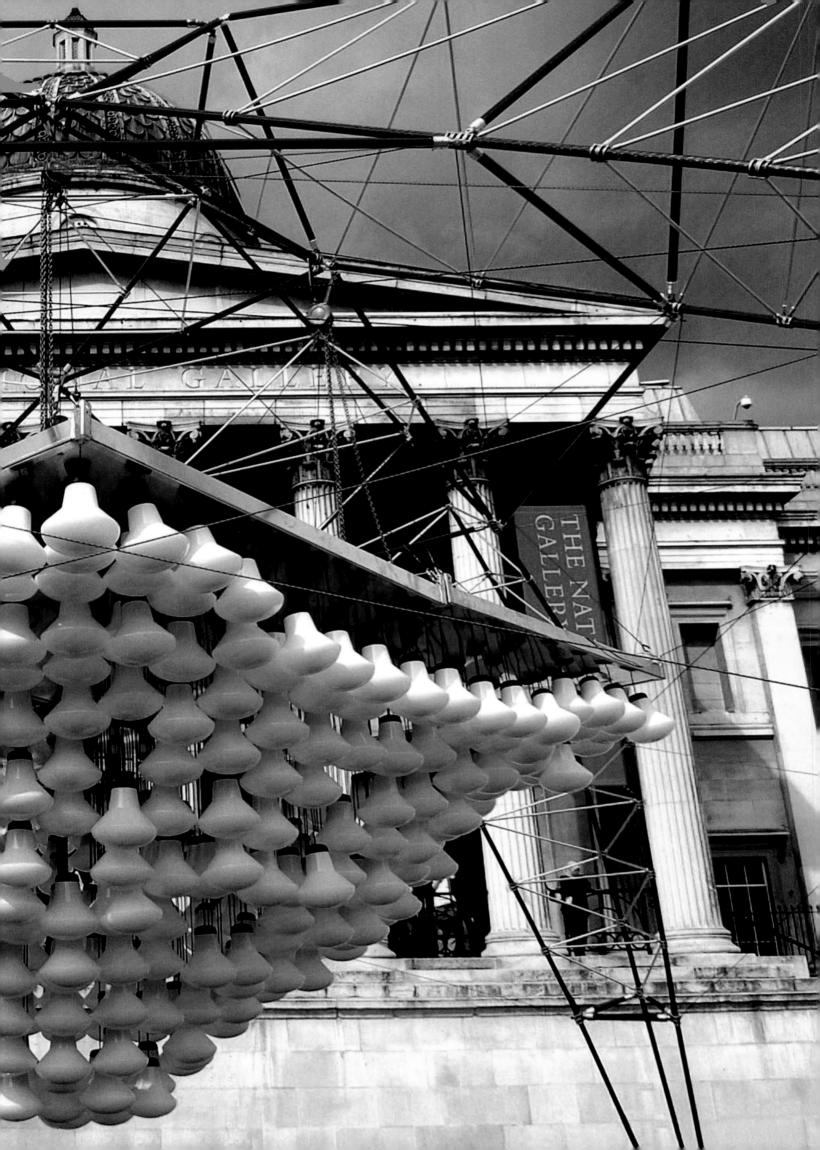

ONE MAN
B(R)AND

The Instruments of Tom Dixon
Angela Rui

Entering Tom Dixon's world means embracing the vibrant energy of a 1980s London where youthful freshness was reacting creatively to the severe recession that was numbing the country's productive forces, and that saw a great rise in the number of strikes, the unemployment rate and bankruptcies. Indeed, in 1979, Great Britain was emerging from what went down in history, to paraphrase Shakespeare, as the "winter of discontent." Inflation was regularly in double figures, the country was going through a depression and would get over the financial collapse light years away from the wealthy and carefree glamour of the sixties. *London's burning!*, the eighties punk group The Clash sang: heaps of trash were piling up along the streets of London because of the rubbish collectors' strike, electricity was rationed, there was a three-day working week. As always happens in times of crisis, those years bred the cultural fortune of the London we know of today, forging all the nonchalant and spontaneous talent of the twenty-year-olds who were revolutionizing and permeating music, art, design and architecture, putting themselves in the front line with the reckless courage of people who know they have nothing to lose.

At the time, Tom Dixon was that rather laid-back young man who would tell you he dealt with graphics and made a living as a colourist for cartoons. Born in 1959 in Sfax in Tunisia, from an English father and Franco-Latvian mother, he grew up in London, where he would only ride around seated on the saddle of his inseparable motorcycle.

But at the age of twenty, forced by a nasty accident to a few months of calm and isolation, he understood once and for all that his recent enrolment at the Chelsea College of Art & Design was not the right choice for him.

Tom Dixon preferred the chaos that was overrunning the British metropolis; that was where all the energy of an ongoing change could be felt, change of a postmodern kind. He played in the band Funkapolitan and the lines of his bass guitar were synchronized with the fast and repetitive *Brit funk*, the cutting and syncopated riffs constructed on short, repetitive, sweet melodies were the accompaniment "as time went by," much like the title of their big hit: *As The Time Goes By*. The rhythms and the liveliness of the London music scene in the early eighties were authentic, free from inhibition and sophistication.

Acting just like a rock star, Tom Dixon lived by night, working for a few years as a PR for the best nightclubs, and organizing huge parties where all was permitted in the old abandoned industrial warehouses. A little out of a sense of boredom, a little out of necessity, but above all out of passion, he taught himself iron welding in his free time during the daytime. A decisive experience, seeing that he still recalls it today: "I became aware that, with a small amount of knowledge, fire and some metal, I could make almost anything." It was the same syndrome that gripped his contemporary Ron Arad in those very same years in London and involving the same material—metal—despite the fact that Arad's work is quite different from Dixon's.

This type of activity would definitely direct Tom Dixon's entry into the world of design; for some time he would leave the London nights, though without ever abandoning their rhythm. The riffs of the bass, their brevity and tension, were converted into an oscillating material susceptible to "instantaneous" working like iron, which is forged, shaped as soon as it is hot, and from which it is possible to build new objects by "improvising," or go back to the material when the result is not convincing. There is repetition in the gestures, fleetingness in the execution, recovery in the material, but in particular there is the discovery of a world where it is possible to *make things* without first having to draw them. Fascinated by the fact of being able to build objects quickly "that stand up alone" (here we have the fascination with creation), the young Dixon dedicated himself to his "metallic composi-

tions" with increasing involvement, excited by the
happy cross-check of having found an intrinsically
flexible and tolerant means, suited to his impatient
and chaotic nature. Tom Dixon does not work wood
patiently, he does not produce earthenware that
needs a second phase and long baking times. He
says that's not for him.

This is the point: making things, not the thing. More
fascinated by the performative material than by
the urgency of a discourse on design culture, Tom
Dixon's work can be summed up in the search for
an agreement within which the material resounds,
and for which he turns out to be the only executor.
A rough ride, as he would say, or a "barbaric" one as

Baricco would write, which without great theories searches in the objectivity of a harsh language, because it is rough, reduced to its minimum terms and to the maximum pace of execution. But at the same time the materials used by Tom Dixon, which are mostly objects that are expressed as single components, become narrative.

As the most recent products will confirm, Dixon's materials are the fruit of a stress applied to the productive process of the material itself; glass is always a full inside which to drown lamps, plastics are hand-woven directly from the still-warm filament, thin sheets of metal are pressed and 'vacuum' forged. In short, even when Dixon collaborates with today's highly productive technologies, he does so without abandoning that maniacal pleasure that is the experiment and that is born from the improvisation, in which the production methodologies enter the system as a dimension totally internal to the creative process, which does not develop aesthetic results by means of a benchmark or a mediation, but directly absorbs them in the project's expression.

However, we should not forget that London in the early eighties was also the place where what we now call *New British Sculpture* was born, consecrated in 1981 with the show *Objects and Sculpture* held at the Institute of Contemporary Arts (ICA) in London. The new British sculpture was expressed through industrial materials, waste products, it represented the appearance of a new desecrating climate, a new energy, perceptible in Great Britain, which worked on the search for a new consciousness and relationship with the real world.

Urban culture, obsolescence, consumer proliferation, but also seduction, eroticism of the surface/skin. Tony Cragg, Grenville Davey, Richard Deacon, Anish Kapoor, Anthony Gormley are artists that have made of (rough) material and the process of manipulation the fundaments of their own work. All remaining very defined and distinct personalities, they make of this return to the dramatic and narrative contact with the material the focal point on which to revive the artistic debate. Schools such as St. Martin's School of Art and the Royal College of Art, today esteemed as the best institutes in which to learn to "make" art, have always collaborated towards the pragmatic inclination of their statutes. Seen as an educational *milieu*, it is not surprising that many of these sculptors continue to personally carry out their works, using techniques that do not call for a high degree of specialization, as well as manageable, familiar and generally fairly inexpensive materials.

Moving in the same direction are designers like Tom Dixon, Nigel Coates and the previously mentioned Ron Arad, who in the same year appears among the founders of One Off, both a workshop and showroom, an experimental laboratory for design showcasing the works of avant-garde London's designers.

Tom Dixon is essentially a *self-made man*: after the first series of welded items included in the collections of the London group *Creative Salvage*, he was contacted in 1985 by the well-known talent scout Giulio Cappellini, who went to see him at his studio/workshop and who immediately supported him in the realization and production of objects that would launch him as the *enfant prodige* of international design. But although the Italian experience would give him great visibility right away, the young Tom Dixon decided to continue his solitary work with healthy unconsciousness and great optimism.

A designer with elevated commercial insight, he not only took an interest in the design of his own pieces, but in particular in the fine-tuning of a productive and sales system that allowed him not to come down to compromises. He had made a name for himself by now; only the earnings were missing. In 1989 he set up Space, which at first was the studio destined to the series production of metal furniture and the design of sets and commercial interiors. Only a few years later the laboratory developed further when he opened Space Shop, a space dedicated to the sale of his own products and those of a few other designers, situated in All Saints Road, in Notting Hill, at the time a cosmopolitan quarter, a sort of "understatement" of the city.

In short, Tom Dixon's fortune is the result of an al-chemical formula obtained thanks to several co-incidences, where the British crisis was the chance to start from scratch, without historical legacies, within the artistic dimension of London design that was developing in the art academies. Here—more than marketing and technology—individualism was taught as a necessary factor of expression, to give breath to designers who worked in a territory, radically different from that of Italy, in which the lack of a company network inside which to find one's own interlocutor was, and still is, very strong. From here on, Tom Dixon's progression, also acceler-ated thanks to his appointment as art director of important international companies, would follow a pattern whose peak has not yet be seen. And beneath the surface there remains a long, infinite, enigmatic bass guitar riff that continues to reverber-ate in the materials signed by Tom Dixon.

Tom Dixon. Full Stop.
Davide Fabio Colaci

Tom Dixon. Each time his name is uttered we fall into an ambiguous trap, so it is necessary to specify right away whether we are referring to the company that bears his name, and that underlines his superb individuality by putting a nice big full stop after his surname, or whether we are referring to the designer (the one without the full stop), an *à la page* character of undoubted international fame. This ambivalent nature, between *brand* and individual, between market and personality, gives back to Tom Dixon the right value of realist explorer, a bit on the cynical side, of the culture of the contemporary project.

Tracing out his portrait means reflecting on his role as designer today and on the need to forge a recognizable universe by way of a personal point of view of the world, overcoming the distinction between designer and entrepreneur. This condition, which seems to release his strong creative energy, is the only one to survive in the complex globalized market where demand and consumption never reach a definitive equilibrium.

Tom Dixon's professional profile can thus be read as one of the most accomplished expressions of the global designer, not only for the design quality of his chairs or his lamps, but for the capacity to interpret himself with values and behaviours that his goods channel by crossing the market. It is not just a question of expressing his own poetics through an aesthetic that adheres to the tastes of society, but there is a need, which for Tom Dixon seems to be inscribed in his DNA, to embrace strategy, com-munication and promotion as an integral part of the project.

This "likely baronet" of English design is unable to make himself recognizable through a linear and continuous language. The investigation into the expressive capacity of the material leads him to build a universe made of fragments, pieces, all dif-ferent from one another but all tied to a Brit soul. Through a sort of pleasant nonchalance and with sarcasm akin to that of Harold Pinter, Tom Dixon seems to dispel the daily stereotypes about the petty bourgeois customs of an England so far and yet so close to contemporary design.

The only interpreter of his own destiny, everything he does he self-produces: from his objects to his publications (which he always writes himself) to the advertising campaigns and the company magazines. It all started in 1994 with the found-ing of Eurolounge, a company dedicated to the realization of plastic products, set up after a long and failed investigation in the search for the right productive interlocutor, and that would "bring to light" Jack, an informal chair that has become the icon of Dixon's work. The subsequent artistic direc-tion of an important and popular company like the Swedish Artek (historically linked to the figure of Alvar Aalto) and the cooperation with the French distribution company Habitat, have led Tom Dixon to internalize that entrepreneurial management capacity of his own creative personality.

The Tom Dixon showroom in Portobello Dock, West London

Black and white Jack Lights, 2010

But making of his own "rock and roll" attitude a personal, almost biological need, pushes the figure of Tom Dixon to elaborate modernity and the project in an exclusive way. We can see in him an aptitude for riding—with irony—that long wave of change that in Thatcherite England did not cease updating and autonomously regenerating the cultural habitat of a country in transition. Just like what happens for fashion and music, which from street culture draw the most interesting stimuli for their own change, also for Tom Dixon the world has become his true reference, a sort of litmus paper ready to highlight and interpret the city, items, objects, processes, textures, materials, machines, men, animals, behaviours. How-

ever much he tries to speak of this in the publication *The Interior World of Tom Dixon,* some conceptual positions vis-à-vis the culture of the project abandon the themes and cultural meanings that are too complex to attract the attention of a society that is highly sensitive to change, to fashions and to the contemporary aesthetic. There has not been a declared critical component in his work, even if his most important ideological choice is indeed represented by the foundation of the homonymous brand "Tom Dixon." Although promoting products through one's own person and vice versa, without ceasing to work for other companies or productions, is a rapidly growing phenomenon, it seems that for

Dixon it was a natural evolution of that capacity of "public relations man" that had made him popular in the London by night of the eighties.

The company Tom Dixon Ltd was set up in 2002 with the aim of redefining the scenario of British design by manufacturing products for lighting and furnishings, which would have immediate commercial success, and that today are sold in over sixty countries. Dixon soon manages to intercept the potential of the consolidated computer technologies and the crucial role that communication and the new media can play in launching a brand, elaborating a commercial strategy as a true and proper unstoppable machine. He does not even miss a single trade fair

or any event in his honour, the ever-presence of his brand surpasses his own physical presence; often laid-back during interviews and shy in his worldly appearances, he presents himself like a real rock star indeed, elegantly casual, bothered by the weight of his fame as a public figure. His transfers occur like itinerant musical tours, often with motorbike in tow, where the chance to be able to produce something is never lacking, and where the festival appearance of the great trade fair gatherings tries to be a participative event where the people can, besides browse around, create and buy. Just as with Flash Factory, presented during the 2010 Furniture Fair, where the visitors could even build

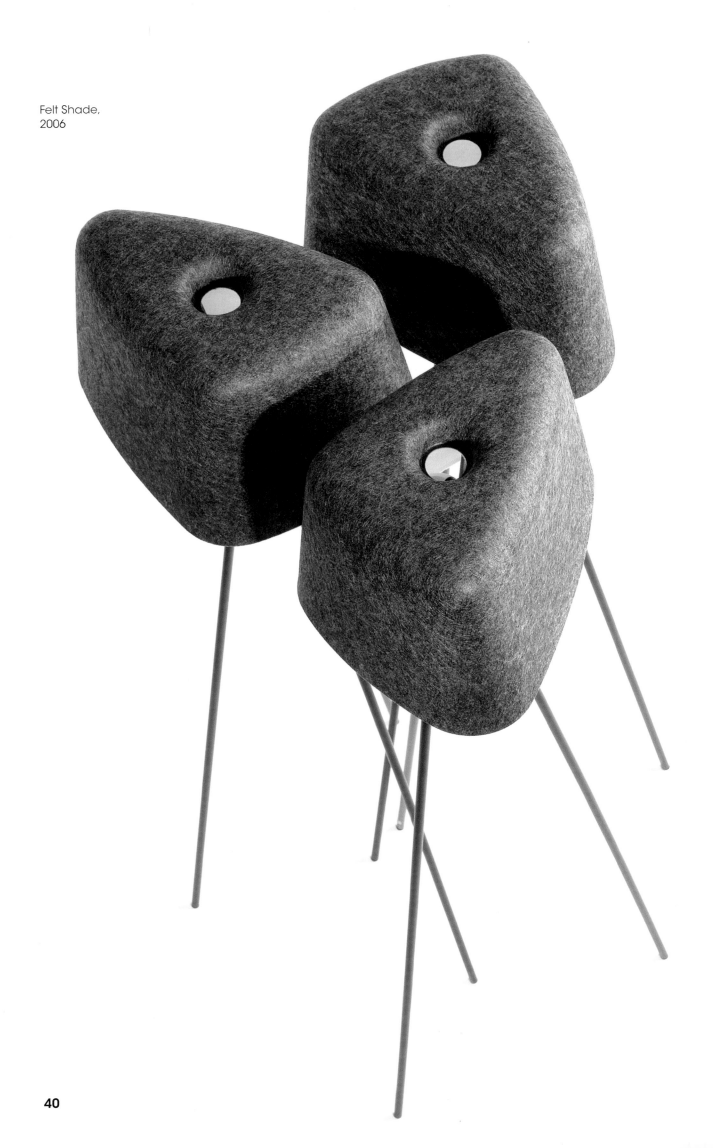

Felt Shade,
2006

Fluoro Floor Light,
2008

pp. 42-43
The Bombay Sapphire
Stretch in Trafalgar Square,
London, 2005

and assemble their own product with the help of factory workers, Tom's adepts in aseptic working overalls. In 2010 the doors of his first single-brand shop opened in Portobello Dock, converting a Victorian ex-warehouse into a place halfway between concept store and showroom, hosting the whole range of lamps and objects of his own production, and deciding at the same time to host the works of other highly selected international designers, such as Piet Hein Eek and many others.

Inside the company the *Design Research Studio* starts to take shape; this is the professional rib managed by Tom Dixon and made up of young talents of internal design, whose synergy between the furnishing product and the construction of a spatiality branded "Tom Dixon." produces interiors like full-fledged brand furnishings. Molecules that through the reiteration of the product are inserted in the best developed strand of interior design reconfiguring from "the inside" pieces of the city. Specializing in lounges, bistros, concept stores, social clubs, bars, restaurants of the upper class, we see all the places of a contemporary society bound to the search for one's own *lifestyle*, metaphor of the decadence of a contemporary London all focused around the search for models, each one different and always renewing themselves. These ambients are often *recherché*, fashionable, suited to a season and, as in the world of fashion, ready to be rethought for a new collection. The quantity of commercialized furnishings, over eighty or so in less than one decade, not only declares a creative exuberance linked to the character of the person, but shows a desire to keep inventing new solutions for us all the time, even transitory ones, for the contemporary design scenario.

Catalogue of Objects

MIRROR BALL

SPIN FLOOR
CANDELABRA

FELT SHADE

RUBBER BAND CHAIR

S-CHAIR

PYLON CHAIR

FRESH FAT CHAIR

EXTRUDED CHAIR

1991 | 1992 | 1994 | 2004

BIRD CHAISE LONGUE

JACK

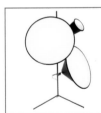

CONE LIGHT
& TRIPOD STAND

THE BOMBAY SAPPHIRE
STRETCH

SPIN TABLE CANDELABRA

LINK EASY CHAIR

THE GREAT LIGHT
GIVEAWAY

SLAB CHAIR

CAGE LIGHT

FAN CHAIR

BLOW LIGHT - COPPER

SLAB BENCH
& DINING TABLE

WINGBACK CHAIR
& FOOTSTOOL

VOID LIGHT - COPPER

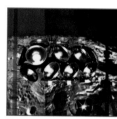

BULB CHANDELIER - WIDE

PRESSED GLASS LIGHTS -
BEAD & TOP

FLAME CUT SERIES

WINGBACK SOFA

ROCK TABLE SERIES

COPPER SHADE - FLOOR

CAST CHAIR

2008 ——— 2009 ——— 2010 - 2011

PRESSED GLASS
LIGHT TUBE

FLAME CUT SERIES

OFFCUT STOOLS -
FLUORO

TILE RUG

PEG CHAIR

ETCH LIGHT

PRESSED GLASS
LIGHT LENS

FLAME CUT SERIES

TRIO, QUAD AND PENTAD

PEG COAT STAND

BEAT LIGHTS

FLUORO FLOOR LIGHT

CROWN CANDELABRA

The Objects

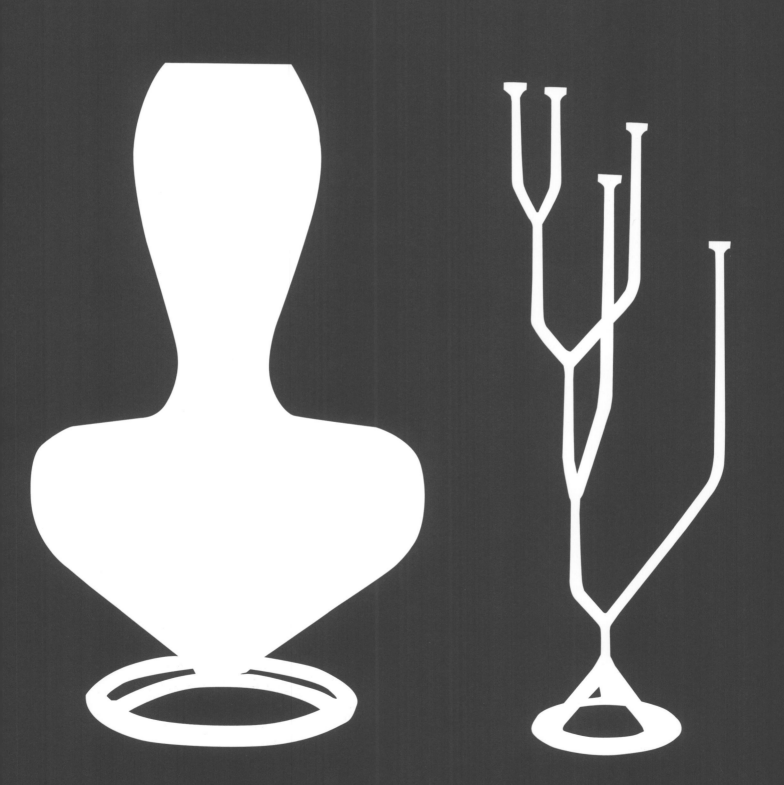

S-CHAIR

Year: 1991

Company: Cappellini

A chair that's like the start of a great adventure novel, an iconic chair that turned Tom Dixon into the *enfant prodige* and perhaps the *enfant terrible* of a new international design, a curvaceous, definite and somewhat startling signature, which boldly and determinedly defies the environment it chooses to fill with its rather indiscreet presence. Virtually imaginable inside a cylindrical volume, the S-Chair rises up vertically from a circular base that's been reduced to the bare essentials, building up the light dynamics of its development. Like an invertebrate animal awaiting new balance the fluid lines create a comfy and surprisingly comfortable chair. The lacquered-metal frame is covered in materials that range from leather to felt, but some versions are in woven marsh straw or wicker. Although the S-Chair is meant to be sat on, for many it's a sculpture that represents the experimentation of a young designer who grew up welding and bending metal sheets in the most unusual ways until he achieved a formal balance bordering on the visionary. A project that shows Tom Dixon to be an extremely sophisticated design researcher, someone who knows how to use the capacities of Italian industry as a guide for a highly visible commercial project.

Present in the MoMA's permanent collection in its woven marsh straw version the chair has earned itself great critical acclaim; the chair and its virtuoso curves has found its way into the most important books on design culture, and the most famous interior design magazines in the world. It's a must that continues to be one of most interesting designs by a young Dixon.

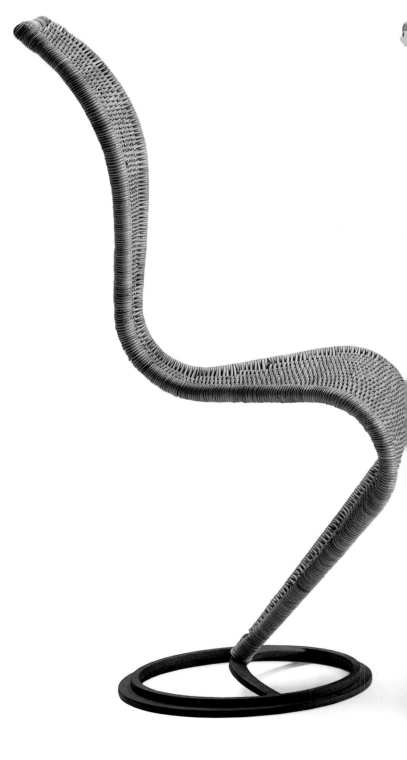

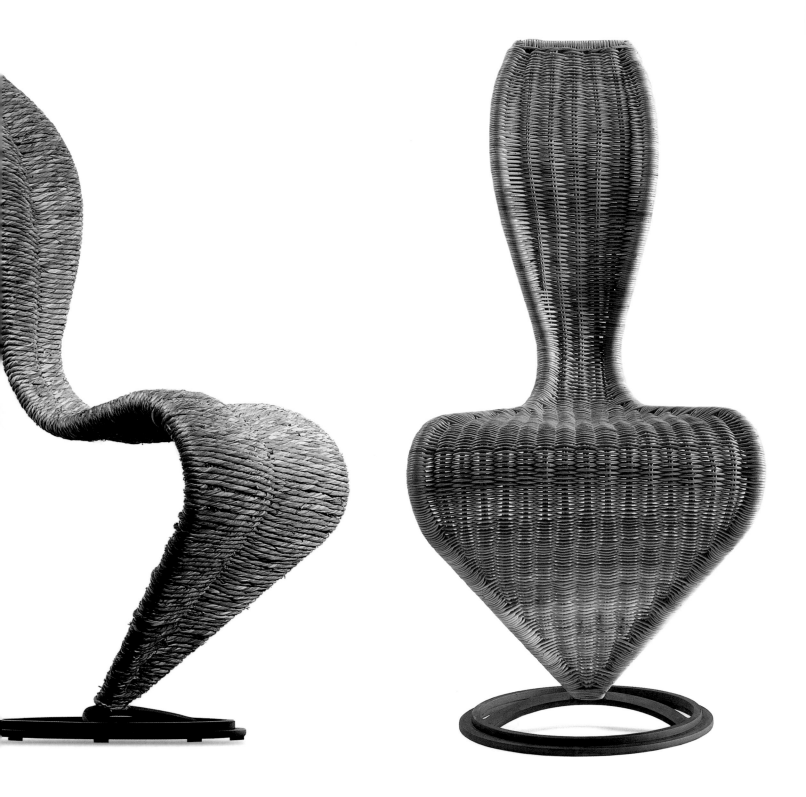

BIRD CHAISE LONGUE

Year: 1991

Company: Cappellini

Bird is a rocking chaise longue, a comfortable, functional chair, that adapts to even the lightest movement of whoever chooses to stretch out upon its wings. Its structure is made of a wood and metal conglomerate that's stuffed with different amounts of expanded polyurethane; the slipcover of the cloth version is completely removable. A chair that seems to defy the law of gravity because it's suspended in a perfect yet precarious equilibrium. A bird about to take wing is the inspiration for the dynamic form of this poetic chair. An icon of Tom Dixon's early works it is the height of the synthesis between the dynamism of those very first experiments carried out by a young rock musician and the domestic tradition of the Cappellini company's soft furnishings. Its virtue and irony are not just contained in the forms and the materials, but also in the name "Bird," which points to a precise vision, the expression of an independent and amused language. It doesn't simply evoke the figure of a bird, but expresses its light movement each time the centre of gravity of its weight shifts, thus determining the positional dynamics. This Bird is a chair that moves symbiotically with the sitter.

PYLON CHAIR

Year: 1992

Company: Cappellini

Just as the name suggests this chair has all the features of a high voltage pylon. It's an object that has now entered the collective memory of contemporary design records. Pylon Chair sheds all of its "heavy" contents and remains a shadow, the reverberation of a form featuring highly expressive content and fine-tuned transgression, which is how Giulio Cappellini, who decided to manufacture the chair in 1992, describes it. Built from hand-welded stainless steel wire and painted in natural aluminium colours—orange, blue or chalk-white—the Pylon Chair dates back to a 1989 project realized in different versions by Dixon himself, who earned himself the sobriquet of "vertebrate" designer, given to him by Fabio Novembre, also a designer and a good friend of Dixon. The object, pared down to its basic skeletal form bears witness to Dixon's originality in grabbing hold of the chance to experiment with what were avant-garde computer technologies at the time, and that in this case helped him to realize complex digitally-aided 3-D designs in wireframe which he then transposed into a geometrical structure. Some of Dixon's preparatory drawings are held at the Victoria and Albert Museum in London, while the Pylon Chair is on permanent display at the Montreal Museum of Fine Arts and the Museum für Angewandte Kunst (Museum of Applied Arts) in Cologne.

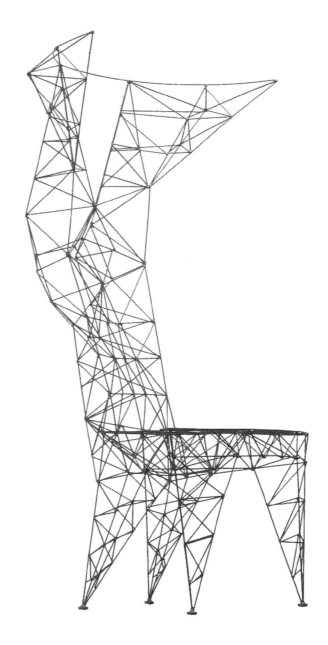

JACK

Year: 1994

Company: Tom Dixon.

Jack is one of Tom Dixon's iconic designs, born as a "lighting thing" that's a stackable seat, designed for easy handling and adaptability with no pre-established use.

Designed in 1994, the winner three years later of the Millennium Mark, Britain's most prestigious design award, and now included in the Victoria and Albert Museum's permanent collection, Jack was the spark that encouraged Tom Dixon to found Eurolounge that same year, a company devoted to producing plastic products and that would kick off his first industrial production.

Jack is made from pigmented polyethylene and produced using the process known as rotary moulding, which at the time was rarely used to make furniture. Although this particular object is quite young, the technique itself had actually been in use for some time, mostly to make traffic cones, barriers, and toys. The artist himself tells us that he invented Jack so that he could explore the use of plastic in industrial production, as well as to promote British series manufacturing, which had been dead for some time. Jack is inspired by sixties and seventies Pop objects and furnishings, and like them has a soft, warm shape, and a deliberately faux appearance.

Jack is now being produced once more by Tom Dixon Ltd in different versions: Jack Light - White, a lamp module, Jack's black version, which can be moved about freely in space, Jack - Fluoro, a new phosphorescent orange version that doubles as a lamp, and a fluorescent version for use at night with no need for electricity.

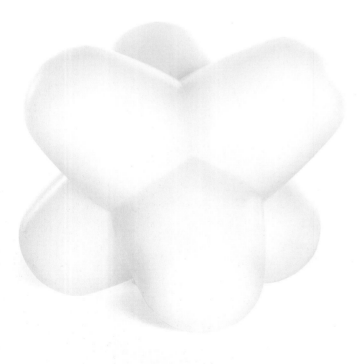
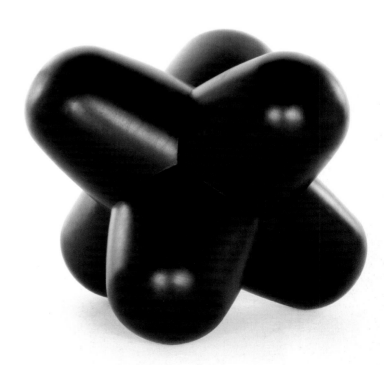

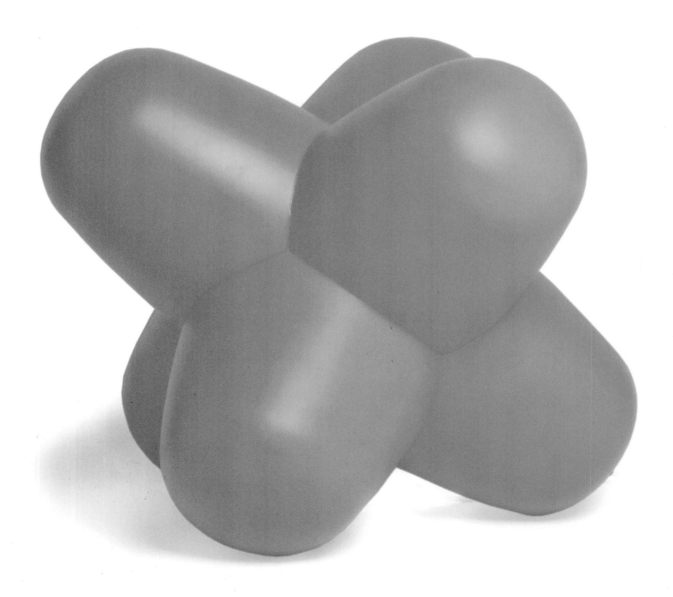

CONE LIGHT & TRIPOD STAND

Year: 2004

Company: Tom Dixon.

Cone Light is a lighting device with a highly reflective inner surface, made using the industrial process that entails placing spun aluminium on a stainless steel mould. This conical light incorporates an opalescent acrylic diffuser which softens the standard light bulb to give a light parallel to the qualities of natural daylight. These luminous cones (which come in two different versions) were invented for use either as pendant lights or lighting fixtures to be assembled on metal tripods. This latest version can be assembled in many different ways and consists of cones supported by a slender vertical stand, whose array of configurations coupled with the orientation of the diffusers create an object that differs every time and that can be adapted to any environment. The light's dry, fine-tuned design makes no secret about its strong formal kinship with the equipment used by professional photographers. The Cone Light Tripod seems to be the "domestic" version of the kind of equipment you might find in a professional photographer's studio; it's a technical tool that fits in with the new domesticity of today's houses. Thanks to the transposition of some of the object's specific features, such as the fact that it's lighweight and that a handy clamp allows the user to change the direction of the cones, the object's configurations are endlessly reversible. The opalescent acrylic diffuser distributes the brightness of the Cone Light evenly and softly, so that it can be adapted to different light conditions.

FELT SHADE

Year: 2006

Company: Tom Dixon.

Felt is *simply* a felt lamp featuring a soft, curvy shape, and made using a process rarely used in lighting and furniture manufacturing. Felt is created by heat-pressing a double layer of material which is then sculpted into shape. Tom Dixon thus generates the twofold nature of this object: a grey exterior and a reflecting white interior. Felt is a sculptural, tactile lamp that gives us English shades of grey with a soft but neat line. Felt, which is only rarely used in interior design, and is virtually absent in lighting, has been chosen here precisely because it is so unusual, but perhaps more importantly because of the imperfections caused by the felting of the surface fibres. Felt is a pleasant short circuit between colour, material and form. A triangular stone that expresses all of its lightness in the pendant version that gently hangs down from above. A lamp made from fabric, both soft and stiff just like a hat; a lamp that's one-of-a-kind and impeccably elegant.

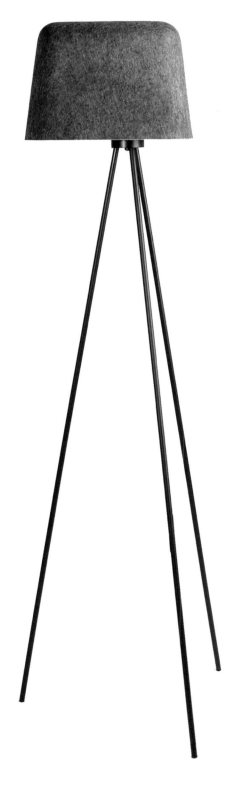

LINK EASY CHAIR

Year: 2006

Company: Tom Dixon.

Link Easy Chair is a very light chair both in terms of structure and appearance. It is really a small piece of architecture made up of a series of metal wires welded by hand and then galvanized for outdoor use. Each "filament" is bent and then fastened, and together they create a seat that's comfortable, open and well-proportioned in its structure. The slender white framework, poetically inspired by chain patterns and sailing knots, is delicately transformed into the very decor of a noble, ephemeral place on which to sit. Slender, but never weak, it blends its garden furniture style with a totally interior and everyday domesticity thanks to its coloured pattern cushion. The elegant structure ensconces its guests but without hiding them, and much like a wire birdcage it seems ready to be drawn in by the wildflowers and plants of a Romantic garden, or by an urban decor. The chair is part of Tom Dixon's Wire Collection, a series inspired by the inclination to use welded or tubular wire to shape resilient sculptural objects where solid material is "absent." The use of the aesthetic and expressive qualities of metal is a recurring motif in Tom Dixon's research. In this case as well, he seems to hybridize the pragmatism of a functional and enduring chair with the traditional and reassuring forms of English middle-class customs,

and he does so by way of the most extreme and poetic use of materials stemming from industry. The Link Easy Chair, which reminds us of crochet-work, acquires structural and expressive force thanks to its ephemeral and charismatic nature.

EXTRUDED CHAIR

Year: 2007

Company: Tom Dixon.

Extruded Chair, 2007, a hybrid of industry and craft, made from extruded PETG plastic that's heated, dyed, pushed, pulled, stretched and self-welded to create new mesh-like polychrome structures and "formless" forms all woven together. An exciting revisitation of the "hand-formed" object, but this time using technologically advanced artificial material and the processes of mechanical production.

Extruded Chair was handmade by Tom Dixon in a limited edition of twelve, which he obtained by running an extrusion machine in purge mode. The research for this object actually dates back to 2001 when, after winning a competition for window decoration at Selfridges on Oxford Street, Dixon moved one of the machines he had begun to perform experiments with—and the result of which was his Fresh Fat Plastic series, still in the catalogue today—right to the department store premises. The operation was extremely successful, and in 2005 Selfridges contacted the designer asking him for another such performance: this time customers were allowed to assemble and purchase the products as they came out of the moulding cycle, and take them home while they were still warm.

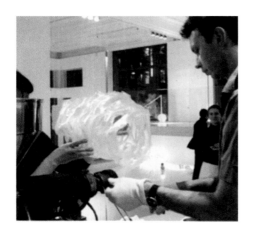 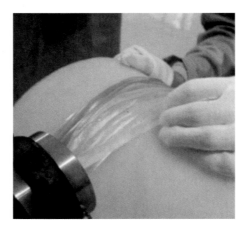 

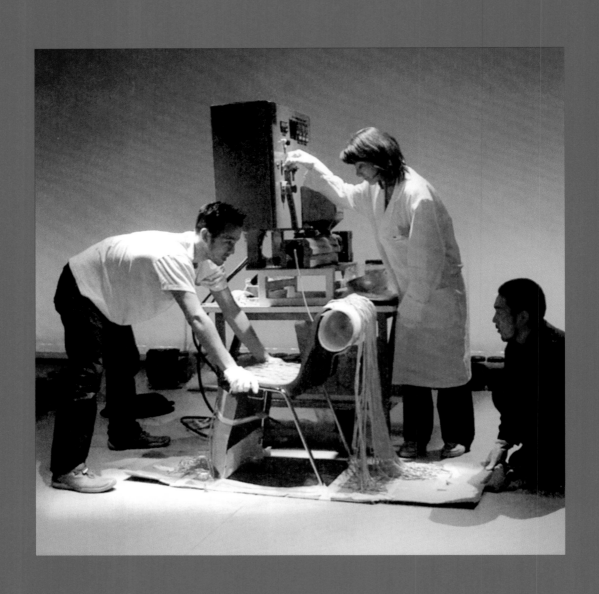

Fresh Fat Plastic,
for Selfridges

PRESSED GLASS LIGHT, BEAD & TOP

Year: 2008

Company: Tom Dixon.

Bead and Top can generally be described as two basic pendant lamps, but the truth of the matter is that they conceal a silent revolution in the treatment of light. For the first time ever, luminosity has its own "weight," massive weight, and glass, treated as though it were volume that's "completely full," is transformed into an extremely resilient material. The basic structure for Bead and Top is in fact inspired by the burning glass bubbles ready to be blown once they come out of the kiln. The body of these lighting fixtures is made using the kind of industrial equipment that's generally used to make highly technological products, such as car headlamps or glass insulators. The collection is created by compressing molten glass into a hollow core mould (so that it can later house the light source) which is then annealed in a kiln to create a robust object. The production does not allow for manual intervention, so small variations such as tiny air bubbles often occur within the finished product. These then become the living sign of a material procedure that makes each piece one-of-a-kind. After a G9, a small halogen light, has been inserted, the glass component distorts the light and is in turn filled with reverberations, thus releasing light that is reminiscent of the weak light produced by an antique lantern. Pressed Glass Light, the family of lights that Bead and Top belong to, is part of a vaster collection called Utility, presented by Tom Dixon in 2009, where the key word is the use of basic materials, reduced to a minimum and reminiscent of industry, and where the idea of the design itself lies in the capacity to create products that are sturdy, and highly suited to the crisis phase that began with the new millennium.

FLAME CUT SERIES

Year: 2008

**Company: Mitterrand + Cramer
Gallery, Geneva**

When Tom Dixon—thanks to London Rove Gallery
director Kenny Schachter's *laissez-passer*—was
invited to participate in *Reconstruction #3 - Artists'
Playground*, an exhibition held in 2008 at Sudeley
Castle near Cheltenham, England, he designed
an "impossible" collection: a table, a chair, a
chaise longue, a rocker, a high chair and a
cradle, all rigorously in flame-cut wax-finished
stainless steel. Maximum weight and cold to the
touch when imagined scattered about on the
damp grounds of this castle in Gloucestershire.
The story is a bit more complicated here, and it
goes beyond the simple idea of "good design";
it is a critical and ironic revisitation of the ancient
fortress—King George III was one of the tenants
here—whose history of seven hundred years
ago is based on never-ending battles between
factions that time after time desecrated and
destroyed everything that had belonged to their
predecessors. So Dixon designed extremely
heavy, immortal stainless steel furniture and wrote
that he gave it a life of at least 1,000 years and
the strength to hold up against new conflicts
should there be any. Also present in the Flame
Cut Series is an ironic allusion to furniture that
can be folded and packed up: each one of
these objects, manufactured in limited editions
of between 8 and 12 pieces, is designed to be
dismantled. Indeed they are the end-product of
sheets of metal bolted and not welded together:
this way, if need be, they can be taken apart and
transported. While their physical weight won't let
them go too far away, their metaphorical weight
won them a place at the Design Miami Basel
that same year, and two years later at Super
Design, a major London exhibition dedicated
to design for galleries.

ROCK TABLE SERIES

Year: 2009

Company: Tom Dixon.

Rock Table is the name of two smallish tables completely mechanically crafted from solid Forest Brown Indian marble sourced from quarries in Rajasthan. Although marble is new for Dixon, who generally explores industrial processes where the material is transformed, Rock Table is actually an interesting contribution to the story told by the designer's Utility collection. One of the reasons for this is the table's intrinsic solidity, the eloquence of this particular type of marble, which was also chosen because it resembles a common stone and is therefore better suited to a series of products aimed at material that is somehow fleshless, but without forgoing the weight factor. The three blocks of Forest Brown that make up the top, leg and base are worked separately and then assembled one on top of the other. They are machine-cut and then planed and polished to obtain a smooth finish that emphasizes the

markings that are clearly visible in the natural material. Rock Table takes its place in a line of research conducted simultaneously in recent years by a number of designers who have chosen marble because they believe it warrants further exploration; works by Marc Newson for the much-acclaimed New York Gagosian Gallery, or Bottle Table designed by the duo Barber Osgerby and manufactured by Cappellini. Obviously without overlooking the Tulip Table, the Knoll company's icon designed by Eero Saarinen in 1956 and relaunched by the company for its fiftieth anniversary. Despite this, what continues to make Dixon's work different from products such as these manufactured in a limited series is the attention he pays to the issue of accessibility. "I don't design objects for galleries," he says, a designer who has made serial production one of the fundaments of his company's statute.

WINGBACK CHAIR

Year: 2009

Company: Tom Dixon.

The Wingback Chair is a direct descendent of the 18th-century British gentleman's chair: the traditional upholstered chair with a high back and two parts to either side called wings usually rising up from the arms. The original purpose of the two wings, which are more pronounced in the upper part of the back, was to prevent drafts from reaching the sitter's face, or to protect the delicate skin of ladies from the heat of a roaring fireplace. This model, which is actually quite outdated for today's hermetically sealed and continually air-conditioned homes, is revisited by Tom Dixon in an ironic and contemporary vein. By covering it with soft dull black mohair velvet to make it less dramatic, and fluidifying the roundness of its contours, Dixon gives a seductive interpretation to a classical, long-lasting object. Conceived for contemporary living, the Wingback Chair is handcrafted by George Smith, a renowned British upholstery manufacturer. Recalling traditional craftsmanship the resistant solid birch frame and stuffing made from layers of natural cotton and boar bristle make this product an object of very high artisanal value. The armchair with its footstool and black-lacquered legs is a piece of furniture in great style, capable of adapting to everyday needs and to every sort of environment. The series also comes in a two-seat sofa model and a wide range of colours to choose from.

TILE RUG

Year: 2009

Company: The Rug Company

In 2009, Tom Dixon designed five moderately optical graphic compositions for The Rug Company. The basic motif for the series was the "television test signal," i.e. the graphic logo typically broadcast at times when the transmitter is active but no programme is being broadcast—the signal that anyone who ever fell asleep in front of the TV in the early seventies would see when they woke up. The Tile carpet is completely handmade in the Kathmandu area in Nepal, all the way from the spinning of the yarn to the weaving on the loom. This traditional craft that goes back thousands of years makes use of high-quality yarn harvested from Tibetan sheep; thanks to its consistency and durability it is one of the most sought-after in the world. The graphic forms of the series strongly characterize the identity of a carpet that uses a dark background to articulate a palette made up of nuances that all resemble one another, but distinguished by a saturation effect and overlapping patterns. Tom Dixon calibrates the subtle changes in colour by means of a design that in the tradition of pixel graphics seems to be a part of the larger design of a potentially infinite horizontal landscape. Blue, china blue and the mild greens of water are embodied in an overlapping of pixels on a regular weave, thereby creating a composition of geometric inspiration that is imperceptible as a whole, but that indirectly refers to the designer's work on lighting and luminosity.

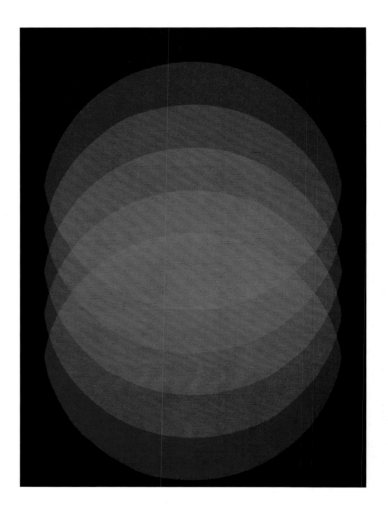

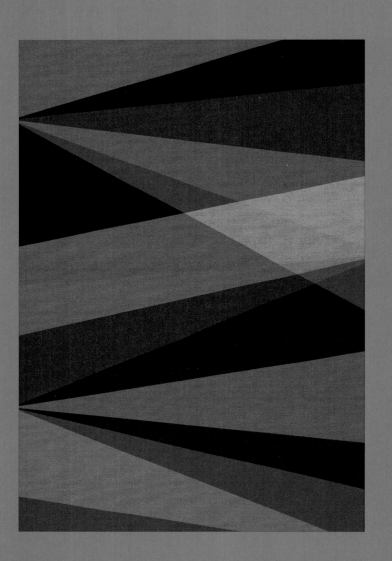

ENAMEL VESSEL TRIO: TRIO, QUAD AND PENTAD

Year: 2009

Company: Tom Dixon.

Three fragments of enamelled cast iron in three vibrant colours are the product that the Tom Dixon brand proposes as a group of accessories for the everyday table. Trio, Quad and Pentad, a name that describes the number of sides they each have; three crazy shards in vitreous enamel to be freely arranged on the table. Small trays featuring shamelessly geometric forms, used separately or as a group, can either be used as a centrepiece or be placed in the empty spaces on a richly laid out table. Cast iron, a strong material borrowed from heavy industry is protected inside by sprayed vitreous enamel left to harden at very high temperatures. Thus, an extremely resistant and highly hygienic surface is achieved, just like what we see in the finest professional cooking equipment. With the usual pragmatic approach, Tom Dixon matches domestic materials with industrial ones, cast iron with vitreous enamel, the solid grain of metal with the polish and the preciousness of enamel. The slanted red, white and blue surfaces vibrate with natural light, giving back a corrugated consistency due to the imperfections in the enamelling process. Tom Dixon chooses violent forms and matches between materials and by so doing reinvents three objects for the table like three fetishes, which are beautiful even when empty, and even when only one of them is used, still play a leading role. Designed in 2009 for his brand, their story is always told as three objects without a context, like three 3-D signs ready to be arranged into a new formal composition, totally independent and unrelated to their primary function which is that of the plain and simple "table bowl."

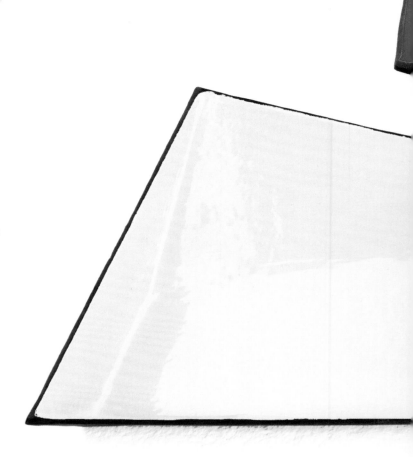

VOID LIGHT
COPPER

Year: 2009

Company: Tom Dixon.

Void, literally meaning empty, is not simply a light but a mysterious object, halfway between a flying saucer and a spatial sculpture, that immediately brings Anglo-Indian Anish Kapoor's reflecting and contemplative works to mind. An object that hides the light source but reveals its power by way of hollowness, material aspiration, that folds and enfolds the luminous beam inside. The effect comes about through a special industrial treatment, where the metal materials are pressed, spun and brazed to form a highly polished mirrored surface, made up of a two-layer sheet

that's thin and light. The reflection, accentuated by a shiny film similar to lacquer exalts all the vibrations and the sparkle of the environment that is reflected on its surface. In this case as well the technological research into the material used led Tom Dixon to push the features of the industrial process to the limit, translating the ductility of the metal into a clearly legible formal aspect. Either used individually or replicated in infinite variations Void is transformed into a performative device that changes in tone and reflections, capable of absorbing everything around it with the virtuosity of its double curvature. In a sideways look to Olympic medals, Void comes in three versions: copper, brass or steel. Just like a precious pendant it can only be hung from a black fabric string that measures up to two and a half metres long thus heightening its oscillating effect. Presented in grand style at the 2010 Milan Furniture Fair, Void immediately became one of the leading objects in Tom Dixon's collection.

Designing
the Immediate

S-Chair produced
by Cappellini, 1991

pp. 96-97
Offcut Stools, 2009

"I was always a mucky little boy and some of my earliest memories involve being told not to play with my food, which I still remember as being a major injustice. What a shame not to play with food, I thought, aged four, when the possibility of creating mountains out of mashed potato or portraits out of toast seemed a better use of these raw materials than simply consuming them."

"Rethinking the use" of materials and objects will be a constant in Tom Dixon's mind: over the years he has experimented with metal, objects, industrial parts all the way to using advanced technologies, in some cases never before applied to develop household objects, which he draws to himself in the attempt to hijack what already exists towards what can be used, really getting into the nitty-gritty of the everyday. Ten years ago in *Rethink*, essential reading for anyone wanting to understand the designer's development, Tom Dixon gave us pages that we could learn from and that taught us how we too on our own could perceive simple, diversified, easily adaptable uses for things and ordinary complements. Dixon's words were: "*Rethink* is about looking at the world of made objects in a different way. Trying to find the riddle of beauty in the mundane. Spotting fitness for purpose where it exists, even when not intended. Sometimes taming the industrial artefact for domestic use. But always keeping your eyes wide open. We are surrounded by extraordinary examples of natural and anonymous designs; those with fitness for a purpose, radical styling, and clever innovation. But how many of us really stop to notice? Anonymous worlds of unrecognized and unnoticed designs are waiting to be discovered and acknowledged by an industry which has failed to embrace fully its ancestry. Do we really have to wait for the next World War to unclutter our heads and blast a torrent of fresh air through this stale discipline? I think the answer lies around us. [...] Spotting new uses for existing artefacts seems an almost natural human activity."

But the theme of re-use must not be divorced from Dixon's beginnings as an amateur welder, a crucial phase for this young artist-musician who would discover in this do-it-yourself method a new and never-before-seen mode of expression that would later turn into a profession: "Luckily for me, I started my career in the pre-virtual world, and my connection with design began a long time after my encounter with the means of construction. From a quick lesson in welding came the discovery of a world of making things without even having to draw them first! The joy of welding, for me, was confirmed through developing the ability to make things that actually stood up. No longer did my primitive constructions collapse when a fatter-than-average punter sat on them. I was getting faster, too—a new chair every day was not unusual. As I welded deep into the night, I was entranced to have found an inherently flexible and forgiving means of making things that suited my impatient and chaotic nature."

Tom Dixon would eventually experiment with materials by leaving metals aside and extending his fondness for artificial material to his interest in the way it can be worked. "I like to understand a material and its properties and the way that you work inside it before I start designing," he said during an interview he gave while visiting a factory that he was still unfamiliar with, where he would spend hours learning from the technicians and artisans there, and where he would work the materials with his hands before deciding what to make. "Some days I work as a designer, but the bits that really interest me are the invention, engineering and marketing rather than the actual process of designing. I think that effective designers tend to be interested in the whole chain. I'm a designer very occasionally. I tend to be on the periphery, occasionally popping out a product which is designed mainly through an interest in materials and technologies."

But there's a whole *interior world*, which is what

Cage Light,
2009

Tom Dixon's most recent publication tells us (2008), that compensates for and gratifies the passion for material.

The Interior World of Tom Dixon is a wonderful book, for which the designer is the sole author, and which garners his endless exploration, an archive of suggestions that view the world from all angles, a world whose story is told by objects, leather, handmade items, infrastructures, related industries, even as far as African tribes and sinking their roots in primitive culture. With a confession that starts from the cover itself Dixon defines what his very personal point of view is in "making" design: "I have to confess that I'm not really claiming to be a proper designer, so please don't expect a whizzy design publication full of tips on how to get the look, or a serious tome outlining what *real* design is as opposed to all the other types. No, this is intended as an insight into what goes on inside me when confronted with all kinds of stuff, good, bad and indifferent, and how I try to categorize it so that it makes sense to me. [...] In an increasingly complex and chaotic visual and functional landscape, this might be of some use to you, and I hope that I can share some of the excitement that I have the luxury of observing in these exhilarating, terrifying and explosively visual times. [...] Anyhow, I'm slowly coming to the conclusion that design isn't a specific thing that is done to products by experts and that can be measured and judged and quantified as good or bad. Instead I'm starting to see it as a process engaged in by almost everybody, on a daily basis [...]. Just like a chaos theorist, I believe that a pattern would emerge from all the stuff we are currently being bombarded with."

And so Dixon expresses the pleasure of letting himself be influenced by other worlds, and when these worlds have to do with contemporary cul-

ture then he immediately declares himself to be more attracted to the suggestive flow of music, architecture, fashion and food, that together create the image of man's present more than trends in design.

This is part of the designer's unrestrained passion for what is true, authentic, what is gritty, honest and natural. "In my own work and life, I find myself more and more attracted to the rough, the home-made, the uncomplicated and the individual or unique thing—whether it be in food, apparel or architecure—so I have called this primitivism, partly because it has a satisfying ring to it, but also because I believe that our headlong rush to modernity—our love and unstoppable adoption of the new—needs to be balanced by some human fundamentals belonging to earlier times."

Some of his most interesting beginnings were born from unusual collaborations. The thought of designing weapons never crossed his mind, he says, but he hates that feeling that "one oughtn't to" design for this or that, which he considers to be an artificially limiting notion.

And the same naturalness can help us to understand Tom Dixon's adventure as a self-entrepreneur, which can be seen in his good fortune in having sold the first chair he ever made—badly—on the same day he made it. "It was a very good feeling," he says with a very British smirk.

"I've realized through Habitat that I'm more interested in business than I thought I would be. I'm probably just not as interested as I should be in money. But I'm interested in the transaction. I could never believe that I could make something myself and get money for it. It just seemed like a dream. Now I have my own company, Tom Dixon. It's a completely new challenge. The landscape changes constantly, often I really feel like I'm starting out for the first time."

Aiming at individuality as an effective communications strategy for the contemporary, Tom Dixon talks about the modern world as if it were directed, once more, towards what's personal and what concerns the possibilities of people today, people who can produce small quantities of "pure" products because they're not obliged to make compromises with the major industries. "We no longer need to rely on other infrastructures to be able to produce our ideas." A comforting lesson, which according to this eccentric figure is the result of working his way up from the bottom, with the courage to do things even without knowing, without talent, as an autodidact, and with only one certainty: wanting to be number one.

"I didn't want to be a designer. I wanted to be a pop star," he says impassibly seated inside his enviable single-brand store in Portobello Dock. And it looks like he's made it.

Copper Shade
Floor, 2010

Slab Bench and Dining
Table, 2008

Slab Chair, 2008

He Wanted
to Be a Popstar

We wish to thank Giulio Cappellini and Rossana Orlandi
for their invaluable "spontaneous conversations."

Front man of the *New English Style*, an exponent of *Cool Britannia*, design *Superstar, One-Man Movement, Mr. Self-Brand* are just some of the soubriquets that have accompanied Tom Dixon's amazing career, and thus constellating, a little for fun, a little for sheer merit, the media aura of this very unique leading figure of contemporary design. The truth of the matter is that Tom Dixon's fame started to spread when one of the most important talent scouts in Europe, Giulio Cappellini, decided to take a bet on him in the late eighties. Art director of his family company of the same name, he met the young talent through Carla Sozzani, a mutual friend and formerly the director of *Vogue Italia*; famous as a trendsetter on the international scene thanks to her dealings in fashion, art and design she seems to have developed an uncanny and unfailing nose for discovering new promises.

Giulio Cappellini tells us that he soon became curious about and drawn to this person who made such unique, very aggressive objects, and who made sure never to hide the poetic and refined soul of his work. Spurred on by this (nitty-gritty) universe of objects Cappellini decided to go to the designer's workshop-studio in London: a fascinating and mysterious place chockablock with welded objects, different types of metal, prototypes, pieces, and not much more. Ideas, no designs, just lots of material. Perhaps that was the very moment the spark was lit: Giulio Cappellini started thinking about turning these "sculptural objects" into "objects for everyday use," careful, he often says, "not to kill the poetic vein of the object itself." Born directly from his background as an experimenter are icons such as the S-Chair, the Bird Chaise Longue, the Pylon Chair: the objects that still fill the pages of magazines and newspapers whenever Tom Dixon's name pops up. Very atypical chairs but, Cappellini tells us, "each piece, although different, has a clear reference to a natural organicity, so that we can find the correct key to reading these chairs, so very different from one another, in their expressive freedom." A sort of freedom that was mediated by a perfect collaboration between the two, which was also thanks to the know-how of a very high-level manufacturing company. Tom Dixon would go live in Italy for long periods of time so that he could personally follow each of the phases. "One of the key elements in his way of thinking and designing is what I call his fine-tuned transgression; this is what allows him to conceive functional objects, but ones that are above all dreamlike, moving about freely beyond consolidated patterns"; these are Cappellini's words every time the critics try to harness the young talent's early production to a specific style or form.

Tom Dixon's critical success was immediately far-reaching and transversal, aligned with commercial success that, although marked by niche products like the Bird and Pylon, continues to be confirmed by the market's ongoing demand for these products. At the same time, Giulio Cappellini's company still considers the S-Chair to be a long-seller, an icon of contemporary design thinking whose sales continue to grow year after year. This talent for conjuring up "surprising objects" ready to become a part of the collective memory describes the designer's unusual start, which Giulio himself explains as something that was stimulated by a great deal of sensibility and intelligence, and the freedom to "go from a single object to a serial object without watering down its essence." When Cappellini, who continues to follow Dixon's work discreetly and with the passion of a friend, is asked if he would make the same choices for the designer today, he answers without hesitation and somewhat amused, "Yes," and confesses that every time he sees him he can't help but remind him that he's still waiting for "a new S-Chair."

From these first encounters the visibility of this young talent began to spread all over Europe, in trade magazine and newspapers, but above all at the trade fairs and promotional events, which saw him as being the lead player in a new creative ferment. It's hard to understand whether Dixon tantalized the media world with his productive performances, or with his parties filled with rock music, or whether the international critics were mesmerized by the understated style of an "English dandy." Little does it matter: in the London of finance and an unstable international economy Tom Dixon seems to be a safe bet (both in terms of earnings and from an artistic viewpoint), a figure whom everyone eagerly invests with the role of "maverick." The British furniture industry, which had for so long been too antiquated for the world of the Web and high finance in London, saw him as a Superstar and a representative of new global design. He began to design for the biggest Italian furniture companies such as Driade, Moroso, and, while crossing the luxury world of Veuve Cliquot and the fashion world of Vivienne Eastwood, Jean Paul Gaultier, Ralph Lauren, Romeo Gigli, Lacoste, he conquered the sort of notoriety that can reach as far as the public at large, even those who aren't hooked to design. This very public, also according to his critics, would be his fondest fans, and the ones who pay the most attention to his transformations.

Awarded an OBE from Her Majesty The Queen in 2000 and a candidate for an MBE, Dixon is the only young designer among a long list of scholars, artists, football players and actors of international acclaim. Tom Dixon seems to have been born for the pages of a magazine, he embodies the emblematic figure of the young and talented person and seems to naturally draw the attention of blogs and specialized sites. His thinking is disseminated on the Web through careful video interviews, highly effective commercial information about the products he creates, his own website that he keeps updated and filled with lots of information, and, needless to say, in the cultural pages of the more formal *Financial Times* and *The Independent*. If his vast popularity has consecrated him as a star in the firmament of design, we mustn't overlook the fact that most of his works already belong to the permanent collections of the MoMA, the Victoria and Albert Museum in London and the San Francisco Museum of Modern Art. Tom Dixon

is one of the few designers in the new generation to be accepted by the establishment, the critics, the world of media and the public. We would not be surprised if groupies were to show up behind him ready to glorify his gestures like in the long tradition of sixties rock stars. An exceptional creative director in the 2007 edition of 100% DESIGN, a yearly event held in London that's all about the latest trends in design, he is recognized for his ability to "reconcile new technology and materials with the simplification of design," as Cristina Morozzi tells us, "integrating the traditional values of objects that can be of service to people"; indeed, for Dixon design is a result and nothing more. In the choice of a heterogeneous scenario of young designers the idea of design as a series of luxury objects is repudiated; instead the idea that "Design is serious!" is yelled out (this is something someone said with great amusement in a video interview). To design for many and communicate this design to everyone seems to be the motto of his media explosion, and this is perhaps the true formula for his fine-tuned transgression: to produce, to design and to communicate. Milan thus seems to be the right place to advertise his products and to promote the designer himself.

Rossana Orlandi, another key figure in Milanese design, tells us what it's like to be a friend of his. She describes him as being extremely talented and bright: "A tall, tongue-in-cheek, exquisite and very British lad who wanted to be a rock star but always answers his cell phone personally and possesses an ambiguous attitude that intimidates yet wins you over at the same time." A creative person who metes out his designs, just as he does his relationships with others, "but who also organizes memorable parties complete with karaoke for his birthday." Because of their friendship they worked together for the third "Tabula Rara," an event that lies halfway between a literary salon and a café which hosts talks, projects and discussions by a number of designers, where Dixon had been invited to set up his own table as an emblem of

Cast Chair, 2011

his personal poetics. "The first thing Tom asked us to do was paint the room where his laid-out table would be located all black"; since then the space (total-black) has been called the Tom Dixon room in his honour, so that there's an indelible trace of his having passed through here. "All his designs are exciting, they're all very functional, suited to a very high-quality market, especially his lights, in this field he's the best of them all." His relationship with industry is essential "even when he interprets the most traditional developments of production, such as the Wingback Chair, he manages to turn the actual process into a fundamental part of the design," Rossana Orlandi says as she looks at the original prototype of the Spin Table Candelabra in her office. And when, in her untiring and extremely refined search for pieces and objects for her "Spazio," she ran into his first experiments in London, she confesses that "Tom found it hard to remember when and how he had created them, there had been so many tests, so many prototypes to find just the 'right one'; and every

time he'd say: 'no doubt that's mine!'" In 2011 he won the Designer of the Year award offered by the prestigious magazine *Wallpaper* (the absolute bible of international style) because of his ability to interpret change. The motivations recalled his Flash Factory at the 2010 Milano Furniture Fair, where visitors could produce and buy limited editions of light fixtures made using digital technology, proof of the designer's ability to pursue the world markets through a reduction in production times and product customization.

Industry, a book that constitutes another key point of his production, has shown how Tom Dixon is an important communicator in the world of design, capable of challenging the world where things are sold and consumed, but above all "the world where design originates." While *The Interior World of Tom Dixon* unveiled the universe of references and ideas of a personal and heterogeneous poetics, seeing materialism, constructivism, expressionism, primitivism, reductionism and futurism as the families of a possible order in design, all this seems to be surpassed by a stronger and more significant production of objects of this "editorial performance." Tom Dixon's world thus seems to gather the largest consensus with his prolific production of objects, events, happenings, showcases, parties and installations more than anything else. Not because of a lack of value or depth, but because his nature seems to be more easily related to the new patterns of a media-oriented and global society that meets with more effective and immediate feedback in the market and on the Web.

Peg Coat Stand, 2010

p. 113
Fluoro Offcut Stools, 2009

pp. 114-115
Etch Light setting, 2011

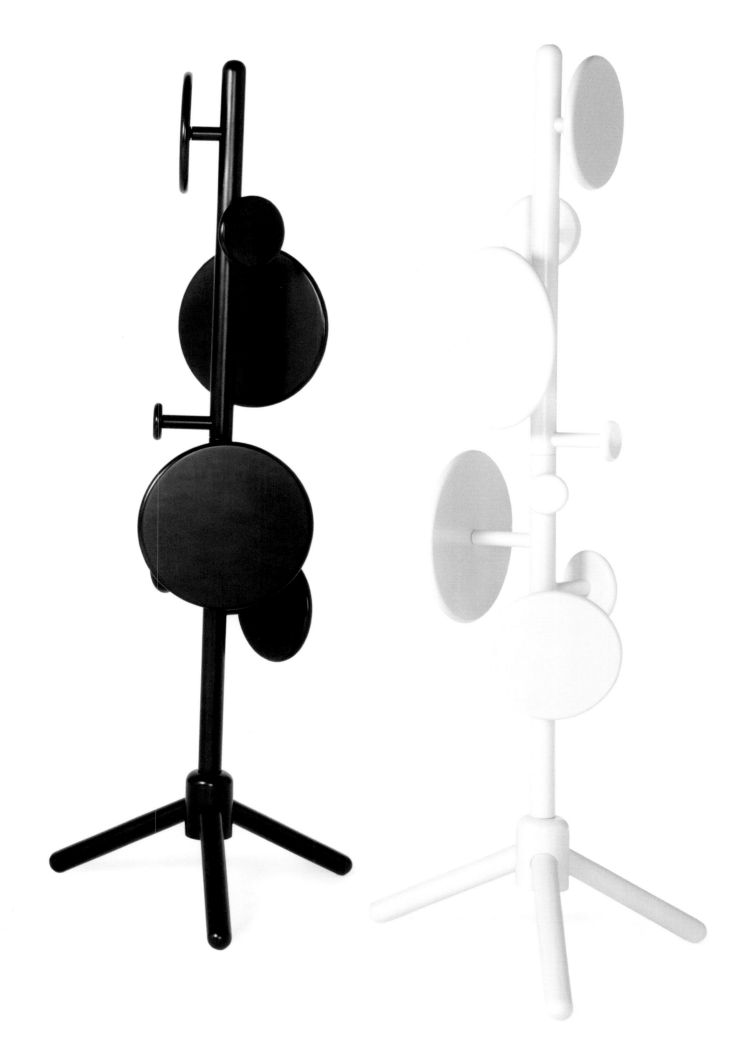

Beat Lights, 2011

Selected
References

Books

T. Dixon, *Rethink*, London: Conran Octopus Limited, 2000.

T. Dixon, *The Interior World of Tom Dixon*, London: Conran Octopus Limited, 2008.

T. Dixon, *Industry*, London: Design Research Publishing, 2010.

T. Dixon, *Tom Dixon Magazine*, 2010.

Magazines

C. Morozzi, "Il riduzionismo espressivo di Tom Dixon," in *The Plan* 12, December 2005.

C. Morozzi, "Tom Dixon, progetti per il mondo reale," in *Interni* 586, November 2008.

On the Web

www.tomdixon.net